SO-CWR-728

We The People

The United States
CONSTITUTION
ACTIVITY • FUN BOOK

kidsbooks
Incorporated

COPYRIGHT ©1987 ELVIRA GAMIELLO AND KIDSBOOKS, INC.
KIDSBOOKS, INC., 7004 N. CALIFORNIA AVE., CHICAGO, ILL. 60645, U.S.A.
ALL RIGHTS RESERVED   MANUFACTURED IN U.S.A.

#1 ON JULY 4,1776, THE THIRTEEN AMERICAN COLONIES PROCLAIMED THEIR FREEDOM FROM GREAT BRITAIN BY SIGNING WHAT FAMOUS DOCUMENT?

USE THIS CHART TO DECODE THE ANSWER. EACH SYMBOL REPRESENTS A LETTER.

A	B	C	D	E	F	G	H	I	J	K	L	M
•	••	•••	•|	••|	•••|	•||	••||	•••||	•|||	••|||	•••|||	|•

N	O	P	Q	R	S	T	U	V	W	X	Y	Z
|••	|•••	||•	||••	||•••	|||•	|||••	|||•••	(•|	|••|	|•••|	||•||	||•||

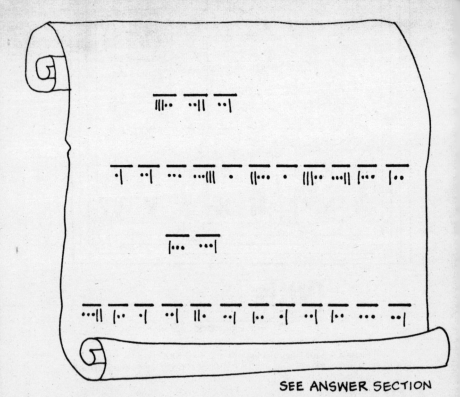

SEE ANSWER SECTION

#2 **T**HIS DOCUMENT UNITED THE COLONIES IN THEIR STRUGGLE FOR INDEPENDENCE. BUT INDEPENDENCE DID NOT COME EASY TO YOUNG AMERICA AS WAR BROKE OUT WITH GREAT BRITAIN.

TO LEARN THE NAME OF THE WAR THAT WAS FOUGHT, CROSS OUT ALL THE B·C·D·F·G·M LETTERS THAT APPEAR. THEN LIST THE REMAINING LETTERS BELOW TO READ THE ANSWER.

T	H	D	E	R
C	E	V	B	O
L	G	U	C	T
F	I	M	O	N
A	R	D	Y	W
B	M	A	R	G

_ _ _

_ _ _ _ _ _ _ _ _ _

_ _ _ _ .

SEE ANSWER SECTION

#3 AT THIS POINT IN TIME, THE STRUGGLING COLONIES HAD NO REAL CENTRAL GOVERNMENT, ONLY THE ....

TO COMPLETE THE SENTENCE, ANSWER EACH OF THE FOLLOWING CLUES AND WRITE THEM IN THE SPACES, PLACE THE CIRCLED, NUMBERED LETTERS IN THE CORRECT BLANK SPACE BELOW.

Clue	Answer
A PLACE TO LEARN.	Ⓞ Ⓞ _ _ Ⓞ _ 19 12 2
WATER FROM THE SKY.	_ Ⓞ _ Ⓞ 10 14
OPPOSITE OF EARLY.	Ⓞ _ Ⓞ Ⓞ 11 4 17
DAY AFTER SUNDAY.	_ Ⓞ Ⓞ _ _ _ 13 6
A COLD SEASON.	_ Ⓞ Ⓞ Ⓞ _ Ⓞ 5 3 9 16
TEN PLUS EIGHT EQUALS —	Ⓞ _ Ⓞ _ _ _ Ⓞ 7 15 8
FRIGHTEN	Ⓞ Ⓞ _ _ _ _ 18 1

_1 _2 _3 _4 _5 _6 _7 _8 _9 _10 _11

_12 _13 _14 _15 _16 _17 _18 _19

SEE ANSWER SECTION

#4

THE CONGRESS RAISED TROOPS, BORROWED MONEY, ISSUED CURRENCY AND URGED EACH STATE TO CREATE ITS OWN . . . . . .

FIND AND CIRCLE THE WORDS IN THE PUZZLE. WRITE THE LETTERS THAT ARE NOT USED IN THE BLANK SPACES TO LEARN THE MISSING WORD.

COLONIAL
COLONY
HORSE
LAND
LIBERTY
LIFE
TRADE
UNION

```
T R A D E L L
L I F E S A
I G O V R I
B U N I O N
E E R N H O R
R M E N T L
T D N A L O
Y N O L O C
```

_ _ _ _ _ _ _ _ _ _ _

SEE ANSWER SECTION

#5 **D**UE TO FINANCIAL DIFFICULTY
AND LACK OF COOPERATION
BETWEEN STATES, THE CONGRESS
EVENTUALLY FELL APART. THE
COLONIAL LEADERS BEGAN TO
RECOGNIZE THE NEED FOR...
FOLLOW THE CORRECT PATH TO THE
MISSING WORD.

START

HELP FROM
GREAT BRITAIN

UNITY

SEPARATION

SEE ANSWER SECTION

#6 **A**FTER THE COLONIES WON THEIR INDEPENDENCE FROM GREAT BRITAIN, A NEW SYSTEM OF GOVERNMENT HAD TO BE SET UP. WHAT PROBLEMS DID THIS YOUNG GOVERNMENT HAVE?

FILL IN THE BLANK SPACES WITH THE CORRECT MISSING VOWEL **A·E·I·O·U** TO FIND OUT.

_T H_D T_

_NF_RC_ L_W

_ND _RD_R,

C_LL_CT T_X_S,

R_G_L_T_ TR_D_

_ND D__L W_TH

_ND__N TR_B_S _ND

_TH_R G_V_RNM_NTS.

SEE ANSWER SECTION

MOST OF THE COUNTRY'S
LEADERS AGREED THAT A
STRONG SYSTEM OF LAWS
WAS NEEDED.

USE THIS CHART TO DECODE THE
FOLLOWING.

A	B	C	D	E	F	G	H	I	J	K	L	M
2	24	6	25	8	18	17	13	10	15	20	26	23

N	O	P	Q	R	S	T	U	V	W	X	Y	Z
4	5	12	21	19	1	9	11	7	3	16	22	14

2   6 5 4 7 8 4 9 10 5 4   3 2 1

1 8 9   11 12   10 4

12 13 10 26 2 25 8 26 12 13 10 2   9 5

24 11 10 26 25   3 13 2 9   3 2 1

9 5   24 8 6 5 23 8   9 13 8

6 5 4 1 9 10 9 11 9 10 5 4 .

SEE ANSWER SECTION

#8 IN MAY OF 1787, TWELVE
STATES SENT REPRESENTATIVES
OR DELEGATES TO PHILADELPHIA.
HOW MANY DELEGATES
ATTENDED THE CONVENTION?

FILL IN THE AREAS THAT CONTAIN A
STAR ✡ TO FORM THE ANSWER.

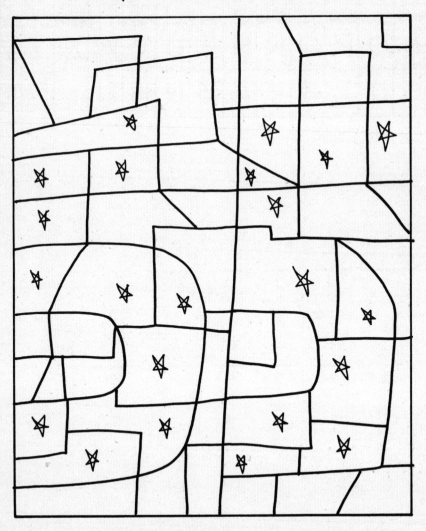

SEE ANSWER SECTION

WHICH STATE REFUSED TO SEND DELEGATES ?

USE THIS CHART TO DECODE THE NAME.

A	B	C	D	E	F	G	H	I	J	K	L	M
15	6	22	2	20	10	24	12	23	9	16	5	19

N	O	P	Q	R	S	T	U	V	W	X	Y	Z
3	17	8	11	4	26	25	14	18	21	1	7	13

___ ___ ___ ___ ___
4   12 17 2   20

___ ___ ___ ___ ___ ___
23 26 5   15 3   2

SEE ANSWER SECTION

#10 WHY DID THIS STATE REFUSE TO SEND DELEGATES?

UNSCRAMBLE THESE WORDS AND PLACE THEM IN THE CORRECT NUMBER AREA BELOW.

AXT	_ _ _ -3
STTSAE	_ _ _ _ _ _ -5
CONTSIUTTNIO	C _ _ S _ _ _ _ _ T _ _ _ -1
IMPROETD	_ _ _ _ _ _ _ _ -4
REPOW	_ _ _ _ _ -2

IT FEARED THAT THE NEW

C _ _ S _ _ _ _ _ T _ _ _

WOULD REMOVE ITS 2- _ _ _ _ _

TO 3- _ _ _ THE USE OF

4- _ _ _ _ _ _ _ _ SUPPLIES

BY NEIGHBORING

5- _ _ _ _ _ _ .   SEE ANSWER SECTION

TO FIND OUT WHERE THE DELEGATES MET, CIRCLE THE LETTER THAT HAVE A TRIANGLE △ NEXT TO THEM, WRITE THESE LETTERS IN THE SPACE BELOW.

SEE ANSWER SECTION

#12 WHO WAS THE CHAIRMAN OF THE CONVENTION ?

WRITE THE OPPOSITE MEANING OF EACH WORD. PLACE THE CIRCLED LETTERS IN NUMERICAL ORDER TO FORM THE NAME.

WEST	◯◯◯◯ 6 8 9 14
OLD	_ ◯ _ ◯◯ 3 16 1
FAST	_ _ ◯◯ 15 7
LEFT	◯◯◯◯ _ 4 11 13 10
CRY	_ _ _ ◯ _ 5
BEGIN	◯◯ _ 2 12

‾1‾ ‾2‾ ‾3‾ ‾4‾ ‾5‾ ‾6‾

‾7‾ ‾8‾ ‾9‾ ‾10‾ ‾11‾ ‾12‾ ‾13‾ ‾14‾ ‾15‾ ‾16‾

SEE ANSWER SECTION

#13 **A**S EXPECTED, DECIDING A
NEW FORM OF GOVERNMENT
WAS NO EASY TASK. ALL THE
DELEGATES HAD THEIR OWN
OPINIONS AND IDEAS FOR THE
FUTURE OF THE COUNTRY.

WRITE IN THE CORRECT MISSING VOWEL
A·E·I·O·U TO READ THE FOLLOWING.

TH_Y   W_NT_D   _

PL_N   TH_T   W___LD

D_C_D_   F_R_V_R

TH_   F_T_   _F

R_P_BL_C_N

G_V_RNM_NT.

SEE ANSWER SECTION

#14

THE CONVENTION RAN WELL INTO THE HOT DAYS OF JULY. ARGUMENTS OFTEN AROSE OVER CERTAIN TOPICS. ONE MAJOR CONTROVERSY WAS...

UNSCRAMBLE THESE WORDS AND PLACE THEM IN CORRECT NUMERICAL ORDER TO COMPLETE THE SENTENCE.

RLAGE	_ _ _ <u>4</u> _ _
SENITRETS	_ <u>N</u> _ _ <u>R</u> _ <u>S</u> _
	²(under R)
ETASTS	_ _ _ <u>6</u> _ _
TCEPROT	_ _ _ <u>1</u> _ _ _
BTOH	_ _ <u>3</u> _
LMSAL	_ _ <u>5</u> _ _

HOW TO _ _ _ _ _ _ _ THE
                    1

_ N _ _ R S _ _ OF
      2

_ _ _ _ _ _ _ AND
  3   4

_ _ _ _ _ _ _ _ _ .
  5   6

SEE ANSWER SECTION

#15 **R**OGER SHERMAN OF CONNECTICUT PROPOSED THE SOLUTION THAT SETTLED THE CONTROVERSY BETWEEN THE LARGE AND SMALL STATES. HIS PLAN PROVIDED FOR EQUAL REPRESENTATION FOR ALL THE STATES.

TO LEARN WHAT SHERMAN'S PLAN WAS KNOWN AS, CROSS OUT ALL THE B·D·K·L·N·U LETTERS THAT APPEAR. THEN WRITE THE REMAINING LETTERS IN THE BLANK SPACE BELOW.

T	L	H	E	D
U	G	N	K	R
E	A	T	B	D
B	L	C	O	U
M	P	N	R	O
M	I	K	S	E

__ __ __   __ __ __ __ __

__ __ __ __ __ __ __ __ __ __

SEE ANSWER SECTION

#16

AMONG THE HARD WORKING DELEGATES WAS AN 81 YEAR OLD WHOSE INSPIRATION WAS INVALUABLE TO THE CONVENTION.

TO LEARN WHO HE WAS, CIRCLE THE EVEN NUMBERED LETTERS AND WRITE THEM IN THE BLANK SPACES BELOW.

10 B	5 T	9 C	2 E	6 N	11 T
7 K	12 J	16 A	1 W	3 R	8 M
4 I	5 Y	9 W	20 N	9 L	13 M
15 E	7 N	12 F	1 T	10 R	23 M
2 A	14 N	11 H	6 K	13 C	27 J
21 N	3 E	4 L	8 I	5 V	16 N

_ _ _ _ _ _ _ _

_ _ _ _ _ _ _ _

SEE ANSWER SECTION

#17 JAMES MADISON WAS A PROMINENT FIGURE AT THE CONVENTION. HE WAS KNOWN AS THE FATHER OF THE CONSTITUTION.

FILL IN THE AREAS THAT CONTAIN A DOT • TO READ ONE OF HIS STATEMENTS.

SEE ANSWER SECTION

AS THE SUMMER CAME TO AN END, THE DELEGATES BEGAN TO PINPOINT CERTAIN IDEALS.

TO FIND OUT WHAT WAS CREATED, CROSS OUT ALL THE LETTERS THAT APPEAR **5** TIMES. THEN WRITE THE REMAINING LETTERS BELOW.

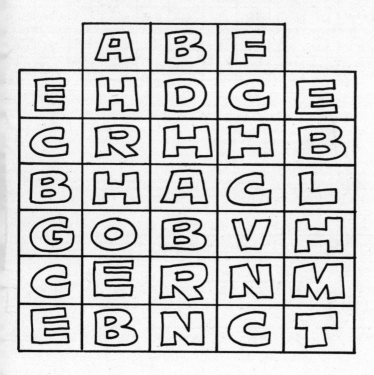

_ _ _ _ _ _ _ _

_ _ _ _ _ _ _ _ _ _

SEE ANSWER SECTION

THE CONVENTION AGREED THAT THE NEW GOVERNMENT'S POWERS SHOULD BE DIVIDED AMONG THREE BRANCHES.

USE THIS CHART TO DECODE THE NAMES OF THE THREE BRANCHES.

A	B	C	D	E	F	G	H	I	J	K	L	M
•	••	•••	□	□□	■■	△	△△	▲▲	•□	•△	□•	△•

N	O	P	Q	R	S	T	U	V	W	X	Y	Z
•□•	•△•	□•□	△•△	□△	△□	□△□	△□△	•□△	△□•	△•□	□••	△••

Decoded message:

THE LEGISLATIVE, EXECUTIVE, AND JUDICIAL DEPARTMENTS.

SEE ANSWER SECTIONS

#20 ALTHOUGH EVERYONE AT THE CONVENTION PLAYED A PART IN FORMING THE CONSTITUTION, IT WAS ONE MAN WHO ACTUALLY WROTE IT.

TO FIND OUT WHO WROTE THE DOCUMENT, WRITE THE OPPOSITE MEANING OF EACH WORD AND PLACE THE CIRCLED LETTERS IN THE CORRECT NUMERICAL ORDER.

NORTH	◯ ◯ ◯ __ __ 16 2 9
COLD	__ ◯ __ 12
DEPART	__ ◯ ◯ ◯ ◯ ◯ 10 6 15 4 8
FAR	◯ ◯ __ ◯ 7 5 14
EVENING	◯ __ ◯ __ __ __ 11 13
PRETTY	◯ ◯ __ __ 3 1

__ __ __ __ __ __ __ __ __ __
1 2 3 4 5 6 7 8 9 10

__ __ __ __ __ __
11 12 13 14 15 16

SEE ANSWER SECTIONS

#21

AFTER ALMOST FOUR MONTHS OF WORK, THE CONSTITUTION WAS SIGNED ON SEPTEMBER 17, 1787.

FILL IN THE MISSING VOWELS **A·E·I·O·U** TO READ THIS.

_F TH_ F_FTY-F_V_

D_L_G_T_S, _NLY

TH_RTY-N_N_

ST_Y_D T_ TH_ _ND

_ND S_GN_D TH_

D_C_M_NT.

SEE ANSWER SECTION

#22 IT SEEMED AS IF THE CONSTITUTION WAS ALL THE UNITED STATES NEEDED TO RUN SMOOTHLY... OR WAS IT?

TO FIND OUT WHAT WAS SOON ADDED, PLACE THESE WORDS IN THEIR CORRECT SPACES. THEN WRITE THE CIRCLED LETTERS IN THE PROPER NUMERICAL ORDER.

COLONIES • DEBATE • ENFORCE • ESTABLISH • STRUGGLE • UNITY

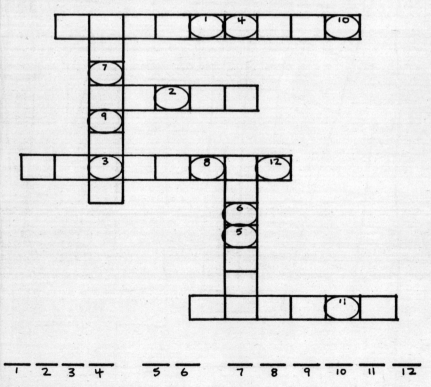

```
 _  _  _     _  _     _  _     _  _  _  _
 1  2  3     4  5     6  7     8  9  10 11 12
```

SEE ANSWER SECTION

#23 **M**ANY DELEGATES FELT THAT
INDIVIDUAL RIGHTS WERE NOT
COVERED BY THE CONSTITUTION,
SO THE BILL OF RIGHTS WAS
PRESENTED BY CONGRESS IN
SEPTEMBER OF 1789.
HOW MANY AMENDMENTS WERE
ORIGINALLY ACCEPTED ?

FILL IN THE AREAS THAT CONTAIN A
DOT • TO LEARN THE ANSWER.

SEE ANSWER SECTION

#24 ARTICLE 1 OF THE FIRST TEN AMENDMENTS HAD TO DO WITH BASIC ....

TO FIND THE MISSING WORD, COMPLETE
THIS CROSSWORD PUZZLE. WRITE AND
UNSCRAMBLE THE CIRCLED LETTERS
TO REVEAL THE ANSWER.

ACROSS :

AFTER "FIRST"
-DAY BEFORE
 SATURDAY
-___ WHITE
 AND BLUE
-OPPOSITE OF
 YES

DOWN :

1-OPPOSITE OF
 EVENING
2- UNITED
 _____

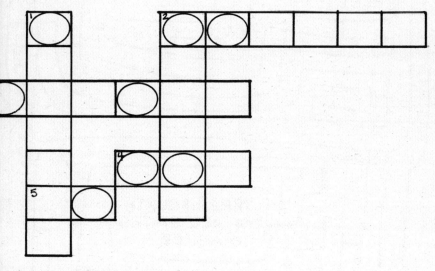

___ ___ ___ ___ ___ ___ ___
SCRAMBLED LETTERS

___ ___ ___ ___ ___ ___ ___
UNSCRAMBLED WORD

SEE ANSWER SECTION

#25 **S**INCE 1789, AMENDMENTS HAVE BEEN ADDED TO THE BILL OF RIGHTS. AMENDING THE CONSTITUTION IS A DIFFICULT PROCESS REQUIRING ...

FOLLOW THE CORRECT PATH IN THIS ALPHABET MAZE TO THE ANSWER.

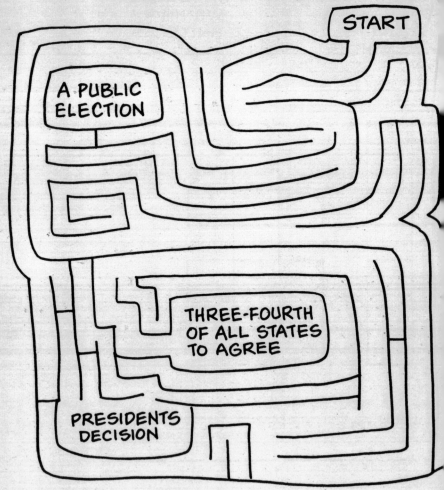

START

A PUBLIC ELECTION

THREE-FOURTH OF ALL STATES TO AGREE

PRESIDENTS DECISION

SEE ANSWER SECTION

#26 **T**HE ORIGINAL COPY OF THE
CONSTITUTION HAS BEEN
PRESERVED FOR ALL TO SEE.

TO FIND OUT WHERE IT IS DISPLAYED,
FILL IN THE BLANKS WITH THEIR
CORRECT MISSING VOWELS
A • E • I • O • U.

TH_

N_T__N_L

_RCH_V_S

B__LD_NG

_N

W_SH_NGT_N, D.C..

SEE ANSWER SECTION

#27 THE UNITED STATES CONSTITUTION IS THE SUPREM[E] LAW OF THE LAND. IT ESTABLISH[ES] THE FORM OF GOVERNMENT AND THE RIGHTS AND LIBERTIE[S] OF ALL AMERICAN PEOPLE.

USE THIS CHART TO DECODE THIS MESSAGE.

A	B	C	D	E	F	G	H	I	J	K	L	M
8	12	4	1	6	18	23	2	7	21	25	13	

N	O	P	Q	R	S	T	U	V	W	X	Y	Z
9	15	11	22	3	5	10	14	26	19	24	16	

10 2 6   4 15 9 5 10 7 10 14 10 7 15 9

3 6 11 3 6 5 6 9 10 5

18 3 6 6 1 15 17   8 9 1

1 6 17 15 4 3 8 4 16 .   7 10

5 2 15 14 13 1   12 6

3 6 5 11 6 4 10 6 1   8 9 1

4 2 6 3 7 5 2 6 1 !

SEE ANSWER SECTION

ANSWER SECTION

#1

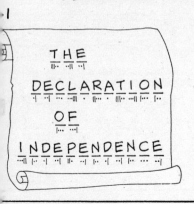

THE

DECLARATION

OF

INDEPENDENCE

(unnumbered)

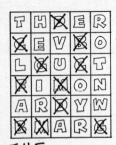

THE
REVOLUTIONARY
WAR.

(unnumbered)

PLACE TO LEARN.	S C H O O L
	19 12
ATER FROM THE SKY.	R A I N
	10 14
PPOSITE OF EARLY.	L A T E
	11 4 17
AY AFTER SUNDAY.	M O N D A Y
	13 6
COLD SEASON.	W I N T E R
	5 3 16
EN PLUS EIGHT QUALS —	E I G H T E E N
	7 15 8
RIGHTEN	S C A R E
	18 1

C O N T I N E N T A L
1 2 3 4 5 6 7 8 9 10 11
C O N G R E S S
12 13 14 15 16 17 18 19

#4

GOVERNMENT

#5

#6

IT HAD TO
ENFORCE LAW
AND ORDER,
COLLECT TAXES,
REGULATE TRADE
AND DEAL WITH
INDIAN TRIBES AND
OTHER GOVERNMENTS.

#7

A CONVENTION WAS
2 6 5 4 7 8 4 9 10 5 4 3 2 1

SET UP IN
1 8 9 11 12 10 4

PHILADELPHIA TO
12 13 10 26 2 25 8 26 12 13 10 2 9 5

BUILD WHAT WAS
24 11 10 26 25 3 13 2 9 3 2 1

TO BECOME THE
9 5 24 8 6 5 23 8 9 13 8

CONSTITUTION.
6 5 4 1 9 10 9 11 9 10 5 4

#8

#11

INDEPENDENCE
HALL

#9

R H O D E
4 12 17 2 20

I S L A N D
23 26 5 15 3 2

#12

WEST	EAST
	6 8 9 14
OLD	YOUNG
	3 16 1
FAST	SLOW
	15 7
LEFT	RIGHT
	4 11 13 10
CRY	LAUGH
	5
BEGIN	END
	2 12

GEORGE
1 2 3 4 5 6
WASHINGTON
7 8 9 10 11 12 13 14 15 16

#10

AXT	TAX -3
STTSAE	STATES -5
CONTSIUTTNIO	CONSTITUTION -1
IMPROETD	IMPORTED -4
REPOW	POWER -2

IT FEARED THAT THE NEW
1- CONSTITUTION
WOULD REMOVE ITS 2- POWER
TO 3- TAX THE USE OF
4- IMPORTED SUPPLIES
BY NEIGHBORING
5- STATES.

#13

THEY WANTED A
PLAN THAT WOULD
DECIDE FOREVER
THE FATE OF
REPUBLICAN
GOVERNMENT.

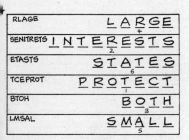

RLAGE	L A <u>R G</u> E (4)
SENITRETS	<u>I N T E R E S T S</u> (2)
ETASTS	<u>S T A T E</u> S (6)
TCEPROT	<u>P R O T E C T</u> (1)
BTOH	<u>B O T H</u> (3)
LMSAL	<u>S M A L L</u> (5)

HOW TO <u>PROTECT</u> (1) THE
<u>INTERESTS</u> (2) OF
<u>BOTH</u> (3) <u>LARGE</u> (4) AND
<u>SMALL</u> (5) <u>STATES</u> (6)

#15

<u>THE GREAT</u>
<u>COMPROMISE</u>

#16

<u>BENJAMIN</u>
<u>FRANKLIN</u>

#17

IF MEN WERE ANGELS, NO GOVERNMENT WOULD BE NECESSARY.

#18

<u>A FEDERAL</u>
<u>GOVERNMENT</u>

#19

T H E
<u>L E G I S L A T I V E</u> ,
<u>E X E C U T I V E</u>
A N D
<u>J U D I C I A L</u>
<u>D E P A R T M E N T S</u> .

#20

NORTH	<u>S O U T H</u> (16, 2, 9)
COLD	<u>H O I</u> (12)
DEPART	<u>A R R I V E</u> (10, 6, 15, 4, 8)
FAR	<u>N E A R</u> (7, 5, 14)
EVENING	<u>M O R N I N G</u> (11, 13)
PRETTY	<u>U G L Y</u> (3, 1)

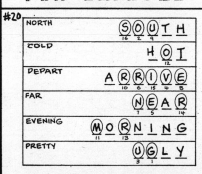

<u>G O U V E R N E U R</u>
(1 2 3 4 5 6 7 8 9 10)
<u>M O R R I S</u>
(11 12 13 14 15 16)

#21

O̲F THE FI̲FTY-FI̲VE DE̲LE̲GA̲TES, O̲NLY THI̲RTY-NI̲NE STAYE̲D TO̲ THE END A̲ND SI̲GNED THE DO̲CUME̲NT.

#22

```
E S T A B L I S H
    T     R
    R     U
    U   U N I T Y
    G     G
C O L O N I E S
    L       N
    E       F
            O
            R
            C
        D E B A T E
```

B I L L   O F   R I G H T S
1 2 3 4   5 6   7 8 9 10 11 12

#23

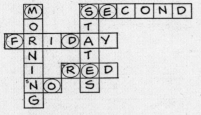

TEN

#24

```
M         S E C O N D
O         T
R         A
F R I D A Y
N         T
I     R E D
N         S
O
G
```

M S E F D R E O
SCRAMBLED LETTERS
F R E E D O M S
UNSCRAMBLED WORD

#25

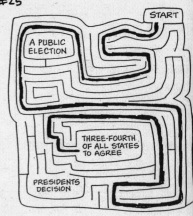

START

A PUBLIC ELECTION

THREE-FOURTH OF ALL STATES TO AGREE

PRESIDENTS DECISION

#26

THE NATI̲O̲NAL A̲RCHI̲VES BUI̲LDI̲NG I̲N WA̲SHI̲NGTO̲N, D.C..

#27

T̲H̲E̲ C̲O̲N̲S̲T̲I̲T̲U̲T̲I̲O̲N̲
10 2 6   4 15 9 5 10 7 10 14 10 7 15 9

R̲E̲P̲R̲E̲S̲E̲N̲T̲S̲
3 6 11 3 6 5 6 9 10 5

F̲R̲E̲E̲D̲O̲M̲ A̲N̲D̲
18 3 6 6 1 15 17   8 9 1

D̲E̲M̲O̲C̲R̲A̲C̲Y̲. I̲T̲
1 6 17 15 4 3 8 4 16   7 10

S̲H̲O̲U̲L̲D̲ B̲E̲
5 2 15 14 13 1   12 6

R̲E̲S̲P̲E̲C̲T̲E̲D̲ A̲N̲D̲
3 6 5 11 6 4 10 6 1   8 9 1

C̲H̲E̲R̲I̲S̲H̲E̲D̲!
4 2 6 3 7 5 2 6 1